*It happened
round Manchester*

TOPICS IN REGIONAL HISTORY

Advisory editors
W. H. Shercliff
N. J. Frangopulo

Night mail to York, headed by Britannia class
70015, Apollo, *waiting to leave Stockport Edgeley, June 1965*

IT HAPPENED ROUND MANCHESTER   **Railways**

John Clarke

University of
London Press Ltd

Other titles in the series
Three Lives
Entertainments
Aviation
Canals and Waterways
Textiles

SBN 340 07260 1

University of London Press Ltd
St Paul's House, Warwick Lane, London EC4
Designed by Gerald Wilkinson
Printed and bound in Great Britain by
C. Tinling & Co. Ltd, Liverpool, London and Prescot.

Contents

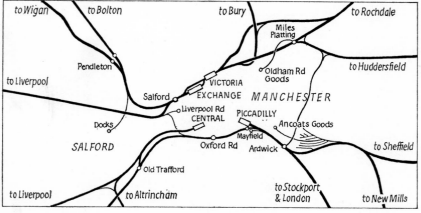

Acknowledgments

Most of the photographs in this book were taken by the author, but he wishes to thank Manchester Corporation Libraries Committee for the illustrations on pages 10, 26 and 52, British Rail and the Curator of the York Railway Museum for that on page 21, the Mansell Collection for that on page 23, Manchester Corporation for that on page 31, and Mr G. O. Holt and the Editor of the *Railway Magazine* for help in collecting material.

Introduction

This series of books will help you to find out more about the history of the region round Manchester. This region has a special unity of its own. A man who lives in Wilmslow may work in Trafford Park, go to Hallé concerts in Manchester and support Stockport Football Club. His life is very much bound up with the activities of the whole region, as well as with those of his immediate home district. Journeys to work, to go shopping, to seek entertainment, to improve his education, may take him to many different parts of the region, which contains a living society. In this series we introduce a number of topics important to our life here, and show how we have reached our present stage of development.

One very important aspect of the history of a region is the story of its transport system. This book describes how a great network of railways grew up centred on Manchester. Many different companies built rival lines and rival stations in the cities and towns. Eventually some of these companies were amalgamated and finally all were united in British Rail. It must have been an exciting time when these new lines were being built with their tunnels through the Pennines, viaducts over valleys and termini bright with new stone, glass and metal.

Now many changes are taking place as railways try to adapt themselves so as to compete with air and road transport, and especially with the private car and the lorry. In this book boys and girls with inquisitive minds will find much to help them in their detective work as they try to understand the origin of the remaining railways and evidence of other lines which are to be seen in all parts of the region. The railway network provides one key pattern of the way in which men have used new inventions in relation to the natural landscape.

W.H.S., N.J.F.

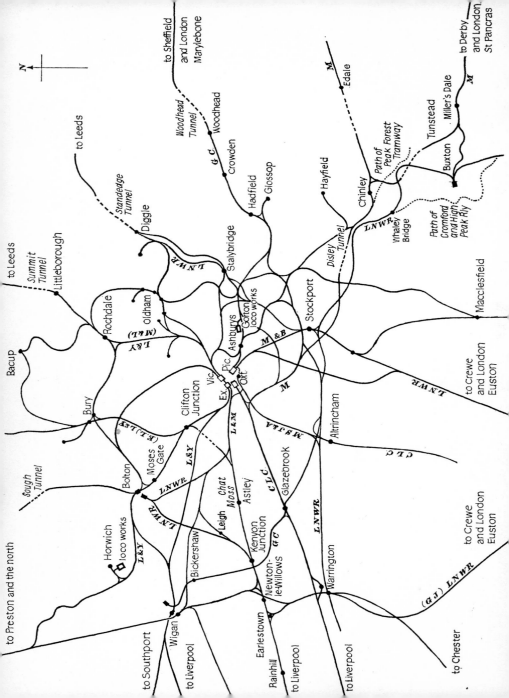

1 Origins

Less than two hundred years ago the only means of long-distance travel was the stage-coach and the roads were very different from ours today. There were no concrete motorways or paved streets. Even the main roads were often so bad that carters preferred to travel through the fields alongside. In fact, the pack-horse was preferred for the carriage of goods over long distances, although the weight that could be carried on an animal's back is much less than can be pulled in a loaded cart.

In the eighteenth century turnpike trusts were established with powers to build and maintain roads in return for a toll collected from those who used them. One of the first in this district was the Man-chester-Stockport road, on the route used by the Manchester-London stage-coaches. Even with these turnpike roads travel was very slow and difficult, and in 1760 the coaches that left Market Street for London took no less than three days on the journey. Overnight stops were made at Derby and Northampton. The fare was £2 5s. 0d. inside or half price for those hardy enough to travel 'outside'. Slowness was not the only disadvantage of the stage-coaches; teams of horses had to be available at various places along the route and, of course, the number of passengers that could be carried in each coach was limited. Nevertheless, during the eighteenth and nineteenth centuries the speeds of the coaches increased. On the Manchester-London journey, for example, the time was reduced to two days in 1770 and eventually to just over twenty-four hours in the 1820s. Twenty-four hours, in fact, seems to represent a reasonable limit for the distance by stage-coach, although shorter times are recorded.

*Manchester in the 1820s. Mail coach
leaving Market Street*

A coach guide published in 1822 gives details of the coaches leaving the Bridgewater Arms, High Street, or the Palace Inn, Market Street, for towns all over the country. The daily list includes coaches to London, Birmingham, Carlisle, York, Hull, Sheffield, Leeds, Liverpool and Nottingham. Many of these coaches had high-sounding titles, such as the *Lord Nelson* to Nottingham, the *Regulator* to Liverpool and the *High Flyer* which ran to Leeds. It may be that the practice of giving names to certain crack trains today is derived from these names of the stage-coach era.

Canals were less suitable for carrying passengers but could carry large tonnages of freight very cheaply at a modest speed. A horse could pull about two tons on a cart along a turnpike road but it could haul a hundred tons or more in a barge. Along many of the canals around Manchester one can still walk along the tow-paths once used by the horses, although many of the canals, which once formed a complete network, are falling into disuse.

Although the improved roads, fast mail coaches and the intricate canal system were important factors in the industrial development of the area in the early nineteenth century, a new and superior form of transport was about to emerge – the combination of two separate inventions, the steam engine and the rail-way. Large, cumbersome stationary steam engines had been used increasingly in industry since Thomas Newcomen produced his atmospheric engine in 1712, which was improved by James Watt in 1776. On the other hand, rail-ways to carry wagons had been in use since the seventeenth century at least, particularly in the coalfields round Newcastle upon Tyne. On these early tracks the wagon wheels ran along lines of wooden planking which prevented them from sinking into the ground, in the same way that a gardener today would use a plank to take his wheelbarrow over soft soil. Later, when the idea of covering the wood with iron plates became common, the men who made the track were called platelayers, a term which is still used for the men who maintain the modern permanent way. To keep the wheels on the track, the edges of the plates were turned up, though whenever dirt packed into the angle, the wheels tended to ride up over the edge and so leave the track. This difficulty was overcome about 1800 when raised rails began to be used, with a flange on the wheel to prevent its coming off the track.

The bringing together of the power of steam and the rail-way dates from the early nineteenth century. In 1804 Richard Trevithick built a steam locomotive and made the first successful journey drawing a loaded train along the Penydarran plate-way in South Wales. Although the locomotive was so heavy that it broke the track badly in several places and frequently came off it, it demonstrated that the steam locomotive was a practicable means of transport. In 1808 Trevithick built a circular track at Euston Square in London where people were charged 1s. to see the engine which was provocatively called *Catch Me Who Can*. It was raced against horses at the stupendous speed of twelve miles per hour, to stimulate interest.

Although the problems associated with the early steam locomotives were so great, the attraction of using cheap coal to provide power was such that other engineers became interested, particularly in the northeast where the cost of fodder for horses was very high. One of those interested was George Stephenson. His first engine, called the *Blücher*, was tested in 1814 and pulled eight wagons at four miles per hour. Other engines followed and Stephenson also made improvements to the track, at that time one of the most vulnerable parts of the system. He devised better methods of supporting and joining the rails which not only provided a smoother and safer road but, by reducing friction, enabled greater loads to be carried.

Eventually Stephenson was appointed engineer to the proposed Stockton and Darlington Railway. This line was opened in 1825, complete with four locomotives and the world's first passenger coach, called the *Experiment*. The first train gave a demonstration of the potential carrying capacity of the new system by conveying no fewer than 600 people on a single journey, although the main function of the line was to move coal from the collieries near Darlington to the quay at Stockton. For much of the work on the Stockton and Darlington Railway the horse was still used, so, being a 'mixed' line, it formed a link between the old and the new.

The overwhelming superiority of the railways over the stage-coaches and the canals was soon evident. The Manchester-London journey took about twenty-four hours by coach, but, as soon as a rail link was established between Manchester and London, the time was halved at once, the rail journey taking only twelve hours. As soon as a railway joined two places, it meant the end of stage-coaches between them. The last stage-coach between Manchester and London, the *Defiance*, is said to have run in 1841.

More lines were built, routes were shortened and in many cases the fact that more than one railway company competed for the traffic between two places led to faster trains. In 1878 the Midland Railway ran trains from St Pancras to Manchester in four and three-quarter hours and in 1884 in only four and a quarter hours. The London and North Western Railway, a fierce competitor, ran trains from Euston to Manchester in 1902 in three and three-quarter hours, and, in 1904, cut even this time by fifteen minutes. We can see how great this achievement of over half a century ago was when we consider that, even in 1966, the Midland Pullman took three hours ten minutes on the journey. There was a dramatic change in 1966, when the same journey on the electrified line between Manchester Piccadilly and Euston took only two hours thirty-five minutes. This is an average speed of over seventy miles per hour, so we have come a long way since the ten-mile-per-hour average of the stage-coach days.

Speed was not the only advantage of the railways over the coaches.

RAILAYS

Railway carriages were not only more comfortable to ride in but could carry more passengers. The railways brought about a great social change by conveying all classes of people at fares they could afford so that travel was no longer confined to the rich. If we assume an average of ten passengers in each of the fifteen coaches leaving Manchester daily for Liverpool in 1822, this gives a total of about a hundred and fifty people travelling by this means. To form an estimate of how much more travelling is done today, we need only look at the number of trains running between the two cities given in a modern time-table, remembering that each train can carry several hundred people, and that there are three routes to consider. (There is possibly an even greater number travelling by road.) It was only when transport moved out of the age of the horse and cart into the age of steam that mass travel on such a scale could begin.

In 1838 it was possible to make a comparison of the costs of a family of two adults and three children travelling to London from Manchester by three different ways.

1) *By canal boat*

	£	s.	d.
2 adults, passage 14s. each	1	8	0
3 children, passage 7s. each	1	1	0
Provisions for a journey of 5 days	1	5	0
	3	14	0

2) *By coach*

2 adults, passage 30s. each	3	0	0
3 children, passage 15s. each	2	5	0
Tips, etc., coachman		7	0
Food for a journey of 24 hours		10	0
	6	2	0

3) *By railway*

2 adults, third class fare 25s. each	2	10	0
3 children, fares 12s. 6d. each	1	17	6
Food for a journey of 12 hours		7	6
	4	15	0

The marked superiority of the railways depends on a balance of several factors and in comparing different means of transport it is a matter of weighing one thing against another before deciding which is best for a particular purpose. Today we could make a similar, though perhaps more complicated, table to assess the transport services between Manchester and London – the private car, the aeroplane, the motor-coach and, still going strong after a century and a half, the railway train.

The Midland Pullman passing Chinley, 1966

2 Early development in north Derbyshire

(The one-inch Ordnance Survey map No. 111 will be helpful as all the grid references given in this chapter are found on this map.)
About 1820 there was a great need for better transport between the Manchester area and the other side of the Pennines. It was natural at this time that the first plans should be for a canal to link up with the already extensive canal system in existence round Manchester. The proposed canal would connect with the Peak Forest Canal at Whaley Bridge and proceed to the Cromford Canal just south of Matlock. (Both these canals are marked on the one-inch map.) It was soon discovered, however, that the construction of a canal would present great difficulties, and it was during the 1820s that primitive railways, such as the Stockton and Darlington line, were showing how success-ful this new form of transport could be, so it was decided to build a railway over the hills instead of a canal. An Act of Parliament was needed before work could begin and this was passed in May 1825.

The projected railway to join Whaley Bridge and Cromford had to cross a wild and hilly region. The line climbs from 517 feet above sea level at Whaley Bridge to a height of 1,266 feet above sea level at Ladmanlow and then down to 278 feet at Cromford. The route decided on by Josiah Jessop, some thirty-three miles in length, can be followed on the map. Much of the original line has had to be aban-doned, for example the section from Whaley Bridge to Harpur Hill appears as a dotted line (to denote footpath or track) and is marked 'Tk of old Rly'. Another part appears now as a siding from Harpur Hill, and between Hindlow and Parsley Hay one can see how the original track has been abandoned in favour of an improved alignment.

16

From Parsley Hay to Cromford the line is shown as a Mineral Line; although it now carries no traffic, this section used to carry limestone from the quarries along the line.

When the railway was built there was little previous experience to draw upon. Steam engines were new-fangled and unreliable. It seemed likely at the time that the familiar and well-tried horse would be the form of motive power used on the line. The main advantage of the railway was to reduce friction on the wheels so that a single horse could pull several wagons. This effect is most evident on the level because on an inclined track the work that has to be done to climb up the slope is much greater in proportion. For this reason it was decided to keep the line as level as possible, following the contours, and, where rise or fall was unavoidable, to use a steep inclined plane. On this the wagons could ascend or descend on a rope under the control of a stationary winding engine at the top of the slope. On a canal the climbing is done by means of locks, arranged as far as possible in flights; it is easy to see how like a canal the construction of this early railway was. There were nine of these inclines on the railway and the gradients ranged from 1:14 to as much as 1:7. The winding engines pulled wagons up one track, using an endless rope, and the load was counter-balanced as far as possible by wagons going down the other track alongside.

The last of these inclines to be worked in this manner by British Rail was the Sheep Pasture Incline, falling a total of 465 feet at a gradient of 1:8 to 1:9. This interesting relic of the early Industrial Revolution can be seen to advantage from the bridge carrying the main Buxton-Derby road (A6) over the incline about a mile east of Cromford (grid reference 312560). From the bridge one can see the catch pit. This lies on the straight track with the running lines converging upon it. Normally the points were set so that runaway wagons went straight into the pit.

*A wagon ready to descend
the Sheep Pasture incline*

*Winding wheel in the engine-
house at Middleton top. The
continuous rope passes over the wheel*

The pit was built after two wagons full of stone ran away in 1888. In the half-mile descent they reached such a high speed that they left the track at the bottom, flew across the canal and main railway line and smashed to matchwood in a field. When the incline was in use, a pointsman had to be on duty to hold the points over in a small hut on the right of the line, as otherwise wagons under control and intended for the foot of the incline would finish up in the pit instead.

At the top of the Middleton Incline (grid reference 276552) is a remarkable steam engine – the famous Butterly Beam engine, built in 1825 and which worked continuously until June 1963. The Middleton Incline is also no longer used; after the track had been taken up through working between Parsley Hay and Cromford was no longer possible and the line had to be worked as two separate sections from either end.

The next inclined plane is at Hopton with a gradient of only 1 : 14. About 1877 it was found possible to use locomotives to pull wagons

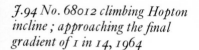

J.94 No. 68012 climbing Hopton incline; approaching the final gradient of 1 in 14, 1964

No. 68012 rounding Gotham curve on the Cromford and High Peak railway, 1964

up the slope without the winding engine at the top. The only present remains of the winding house are a mound of stones at the top and the incline had the distinction of being the steepest running line on British Rail. In 1967 one train a day climbed the slope and it often had to split its load and take up one portion at a time. The road between Brassington and Wirksworth runs alongside the railway and the train climbing the 1 : 14 section of the bank about 10 a.m. was well worth seeing. The J94 engine produced stupendous volumes of steam and noise, although no fast run was taken at the bank, on account of the sharp curve at the foot of the slope, where in 1937 the engine and four wagons of the morning train left the track and fell off the embankment on to the road below, unfortunately killing the driver. After this, a speed limit was enforced. Another interesting curve on the line is at Gotham (grid reference 186584), which was the sharpest curve on British Rail with a radius of only 140 feet.

The Shallcross Incline, and Bunsall Incline, which is now used as

*The Bunsall Incline on the Cromford and High Peak Railway,
now converted into a motor road. In the foreground are two
of the original stone sleepers*

a road, were abandoned along with the rest of the track between
Ladmanlow and Whaley Bridge in June 1892. The reason why can
be seen on the map. When the new line was built from Hurdlow to
Buxton, goods could reach Whaley Bridge via Buxton and the line
already existing from Buxton through Dove Holes to Whaley Bridge
and Stockport. This was one of the earliest closures and the route is
well worth exploring now that over seventy years have gone by. The
area can be reached from the Manchester side by train to Whaley
Bridge where the canal and transit shed can be seen. Nearby is the
disused Whaley Bridge Incline, which as recently as 1952 was worked
by a horse. With the help of a one-inch map the route of the old railway climbing up to the appropriately named Wild Moor can be
explored. This is only one of several routes over this area. Traces of
the old pack-horse route can be seen and to the north of the rever-
berating A6 lies a more peaceful Roman road.

A wagon and portion of track from the Peak Forest Tramway preserved in the York Railway Museum

1796

The train back to Manchester can be caught at Buxton (passing through the same station at Whaley Bridge), where there are two separate stations, evidence of the rivalry between the two railway companies that originally served the town, the Midland Railway and the London and North Western Railway. The large area of glass on the station is a remembrance of Sir Joseph Paxton who designed the Crystal Palace and was a director of the Midland Railway. The glass can now be seen only on the London and North Western side of the station, the roof of the Midland side having been removed in 1965.

Another interesting reminder of the earlier days of the Industrial Revolution in this area is the Peak Forest Tramway. This was older even than the Cromford and High Peak Railway, having been opened in 1796, and it was used to carry stone from the quarries round Dove Holes to the Peak Forest Canal at Bugsworth (now called Buxworth). Horses were used to pull the empty wagons uphill from Bugsworth to the quarries where, loaded with stone, a train of up to forty wagons was allowed to run downhill for six miles to the canal basin. Hundreds of tons of six-inch stone setts for the cobbled streets of many Lancashire towns came down the Peak Forest Tramway in this manner, and it was only in 1920 that the line was closed. If you return to Manchester by the L.N.W.R. line you will see the track of the tramway on the right, alongside the present railway, just beyond the stop at Dove Holes. A better way to see it is on foot and at many points you can see the double line of stone sleepers upon which the track was laid. On the early railways stone blocks were mainly used instead of the concrete sleepers in favour today and in many places the age of a line is evident from these stone blocks, which were often used later to face embankments or other building works and are easy to recognise by the 'hole and chair' outline in the centre.

A milepost on the Cromford and High Peak Railway

3 The Liverpool and Manchester Railway

Between 1800 and 1820 trade and industry in the Manchester area expanded rapidly but transport of raw cotton to the mills from the Port of Liverpool was a serious problem. Most of the cotton came by the Duke of Bridgewater's Canal and the Irwell Navigation, but the canals and river could not meet all the demands made upon them. Cotton and other goods often waited for weeks at Liverpool and when the canals froze over in winter, all movement was stopped. Also, as the canal-owners had an almost complete monopoly, they could charge high rates, the roads of those days being quite unsuitable for any long-distance haulage of heavy goods. In these circumstances it was proposed to build a tramroad to link the two towns, and because of his success with the Stockton and Darlington Railway Stephenson was asked to make a survey for the line.

The proposed railway aroused much opposition, particularly from those with interest in the canals. There was often violent resistance to the surveyors. The big landowners, the Duke of Bridgewater and the Lords Sefton and Derby, organised their farmers and game-keepers to prevent the surveyors from getting on with their work, but by various ruses Stephenson and his men completed the job. On one occasion a group lured away the waiting gamekeepers by firing shots in one quarter while the survey proceeded by moonlight in another. Eventually the survey was completed and laid before Parliament.

The enemies of the scheme now did all they could to prevent the plan from being accepted. They claimed that the new railway would prevent cows from grazing, stop hens laying and that the poisonous fumes from the engines would kill passing birds. Houses near the line would be set on fire by sparks, horses would become extinct, boilers would burst and blow the passengers to atoms. In any case, they claimed, the railway would never work. In fact, when George Stephenson stated that his steam locomotive would travel at twenty miles per hour, his friends told him to moderate his views as otherwise he would inevitably damn the whole thing and be himself regarded as a maniac fit for Bedlam. The average speed of the fast mail coaches was then about ten miles per hour.

In 1825 George Stephenson was summoned by the Parliamentary Committee enquiring into the Liverpool and Manchester Bill to defend his plans. This he did with great skill in his North Country manner; when he was asked: 'Suppose, now, one of these engines to be going along a railroad at the rate of nine or ten miles an hour, and that a cow were to stray upon the line and get in the way of the engine, would not that, think you, be a very awkward circumstance?' he replied: 'Yes, very awkward indeed – for the coo!' However, the cross-examination revealed shortcomings in some of the plans, such as the proposal to cross Chat Moss, a great bog extending five miles west of Manchester, and after lengthy investigations the plan was rejected. (Chat Moss is marked on the one-inch Ordnance Survey map, sheet 101, just to the west of Eccles.) The organisers were not discouraged, however, and after another survey of the line an Act of Parliament was finally passed, although the preliminaries alone cost £27,000, a prodigious sum for those days.

In the days when the wheelbarrow and the horse and cart were the chief aids to construction, the building of the line presented great difficulties and its completion was a triumph hard for us to appreciate today. On his first day the resident engineer appointed by Stephenson to survey Chat Moss, a spongy morass, slipped off the line of planks laid over the bog and began to sink. The more he struggled, the deeper he sank and it was only through the help of several workmen that he was pulled to safety. He was said to be 'much disheartened'! Stephenson's bold plan was to float the railway over the bog, spreading the load with a matting of heath and branches piled layer upon layer to a depth of about twenty-five feet. This was intended not only to support the weight of the trains by floatation but also to distribute the weight over a much greater area so that the pressure at any given point was reduced.

Progress was very slow and the directors of the company were becoming very alarmed at the expense, but Stephenson never lost faith in his plan and the work was eventually completed. The track over Chat Moss has, to this day, proved one of the best running sections of the line. It has a natural springiness which can be well observed from the site of the old station at Astley (now pulled down). This can be reached by turning south off the East Lancashire Road at Higher Green. About two miles south is the level crossing over the line in the middle of the Moss. The sight of a Type 4 diesel weighing over 130 tons travelling at speed over the floating line, at the head of

Sankey Viaduct, 1831

the Newcastle-Liverpool express, is one to be remembered. A wave of compression travels along with the train through the bog and the whole ground rises and falls for several yards around, like waves on the surface of water.

Another notable feature of this line is the Sankey Viaduct. It consists of nine spans of fifty feet crossing at a height of seventy feet above the Sankey Brook and Canal. It says much for the skill and workmanship of the early pioneers that a viaduct built over a hundred and thirty years ago to carry engines weighing about five tons (*Rocket* weighed four and a quarter tons) now safely carries locomotives weighing up to 140 tons. There is another interesting bridge of four arches at Newton and a bridge over the line at Rainhill claimed to be the first example of a skew bridge. It carries what was then the turnpike road at an angle of thirty-four degrees to the railway. There are also important works near Liverpool; as the Lords Sefton and Derby objected to the line crossing their land the route goes through a tunnel and a deep cutting at Olive Mount.

It was on the Liverpool and Manchester Railway that the superiority

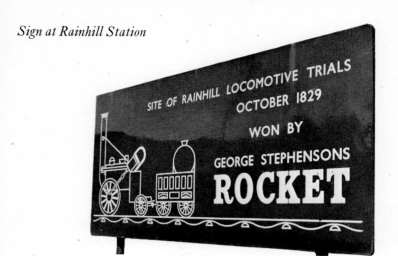

of the steam locomotive over the horse or other possible rivals was established. This was at the famous Rainhill Trials in 1829. Before these, one scheme given serious consideration was to have twenty-one fixed engines along the line, the trains being drawn along the resulting nineteen sections by means of ropes. Among the conditions laid down for the locomotive trials it was specified that, for a prize of £500, the engine must pull a load of twenty tons at ten miles per hour, have a boiler pressure of not more than fifty pounds per square inch, have two safety valves, weigh not more than four and a half tons and cost less than £550.

There were four entries, apart from one, the *Cycloped*, that was disqualified because it was found to be worked by a horse. The entrant *Perseverance* arrived late and was not of comparable performance with the rest. It only struggled along at a mere four or five miles per hour. *Novelty* was the favourite before the trials, but after a promising start a burst of smoke and flame from its interior showed that the bellows working its furnace had failed and halted its progress. The engine *Sans Pareil* was not only above the stipulated weight but, owing to a defective water feed to the boiler, it fused a lead plug and released all its steam just in front of the grandstand.

So it was that the *Rocket*, the entry of the two Stephensons, George and his son Robert, demonstrated its superiority over all the others and, fulfilling the conditions of the trials, won the prize. Both *Rocket* and *Sans Pareil* can be seen in the Science Museum in South Kensington, London.

The opening of the Liverpool and Manchester Railway took place on 15 September 1830, and huge crowds from all over the country came to see the remarkable event. To open the line, the Duke of Wellington and many other important people travelled from Liverpool in a procession of special trains using the eight locomotives built for the company. The engines were the *Northumbrian, Phoenix, North Star, Rocket, Dart, Comet, Arrow* and *Meteor*; enthusiasts will notice that some of these names have been inherited by later locomotives used in the Manchester area. The opening was spoilt, however, by the first railway fatality – William Huskisson, one of the Members of Parliament for Liverpool, died after being struck by *Rocket*. A memorial tablet to him can be seen from the train on the south side of the line between Newton le Willows and Earlestown.

What were the consequences of the opening of the new railway? Even the most optimistic estimates of speed were exceeded as speeds of thirty miles per hour soon became common, instead of ten. This brought the travelling time between Liverpool and Manchester down to less than one hour and travelling by train was much more comfortable than on the bumping stage-coaches. At first passenger traffic was so important that very few engines could be spared for freight, but, although the railway could not immediately fulfil all the demands made on it, its competition in the transport of goods affected the rates charged by the canals as the canal-owners had to reduce their profits.

The effect on society was remarkable; people flocked from miles

The frontage of the old Liverpool Road Station, Manchester

around to experience the new sensation of travelling in a railway train and they returned home eager to have a railway in their own area. Certain people were alarmed, of course – people with shares in the canal companies, stage-coach operators, turnpike trusts and proprietors of coaching inns. Although the Government employed Telford the engineer to improve roads, railway progress could not be halted. New railways were opened in large numbers during the next few decades, their promoters spurred on by the prospect of high profits, and Manchester in particular became the centre of main and branch lines running in many directions.

Although many of the original features of the Manchester–Liverpool line remain today, there have, of course, been changes over the years. A passenger travelling on this route now starts from Manchester Exchange Station and the original station, at Liverpool Road, is now used as a goods depot. There is a plaque over the station doorway to commemorate this as the first passenger station in the world to have a regular steam-hauled locomotive service. Inside there are many relics

Liverpool to Manchester		Manchester to Liverpool	
First Class	Second Class	First Class	Second Class
3 15 a.m byParkside	7 0 a.m.	3 30 a.m. { Per Grand Junction Train to Parkside	
8 45 „	.... 9 45 „		7 30 a.m.
11 0 „	.... 11 45 „	9 0 a.m......... 10 0 „	
2 0 p.m. .... 2 Mixed } Stop only at Newton		11 15 „ .... 11 45 „	
	2 30 p.m.	2 0 p.m........ 2 0 mix. } Stop only at Newton	
4 45 p.m. .... 5 30 „			
7 15 „ .... 7 15mix } Stop only at Newton & Parkside		5 0 p.m.. *2¾ & 5½ p.m.	
		7 15 „ ...... 7 15 mix. } Stop only at Newton & Parkside	

The 3¼ a.m. train from Liverpool starts from the Station, Edge Hill, to which place any passenger wishing to go by this train must proceed to take his place.

* Except on Saturdays, when this train does not start till 3.

On Sundays.

First Class	Second Class	First Class	Second Class
3 15 a.m. by Parkside		3 30 a.m. { Per Grand Junction Train to Parkside	
8 0 „ .... 7 0 a.m.			
4 45 p.m. .... 5 30 p.m.		8 0 „ .... 7 0 a.m.	
7 15 „ .... 7 15 mix. } Stop only at Newton & Parkside		5 0 p.m. .... 5 30 p.m.	
		7 15 „ .... 7 15 mix. } Stop only at Newton & Parkside	

Fares.

By first class train, four inside, royal mail........	6s.	6d.
„ ditto six inside, glass coach........	6s.	0d.
„ second class train, glass coaches	6s.	0d.
„ ditto open carriages	4s.	6d.

Horses: For one horse 14s.; two horses 20s.; three horses 24s.

Timetable, 1842

of past days: an old booking window, station bell, a portion of rail and the original sun-dial of 1833. A journey to Liverpool by rail today is a journey through history. As the line curves to the left past Salford Station and joins the original route, we can see the Liverpool Road goods station on the left. Beyond Eccles the train crosses Chat Moss, scene of George Stephenson's triumph over nature, and then passes Kenyon Junction, the first railway junction in the world, now closed and in ruins. This was the connection with the Bolton and Leigh

Railway, actually slightly older than the Manchester-Liverpool line. Earlestown, further on, is one of the few triangular stations in the British Isles, with a splendid waiting-room used for Board Meetings of the early railway company.

The success of the Liverpool and Manchester Railway was the beginning of the Railway Age in Britain and this new form of cheap and rapid transport furthered the Industrial Revolution.

Sundial at Liverpool Road Station

4 The railways into Manchester and their termini

The success of the Liverpool and Manchester Railway stimulated the building of other railways, and this continued into the early twentieth century. In our area, as in the rest of the country, there were many independent companies. Sometimes they co-operated in a friendly manner, though quite often they worked against each other in bitter rivalry. There was a tendency for the larger companies to extend their territories by buying up the smaller ones and this happened to the Liverpool and Manchester Railway.

Passengers from Liverpool and Manchester could travel to London by the Grand Junction Railway; it ran to Birmingham where passengers changed for London on to the London and Birmingham Railway. In 1845 the Liverpool and Manchester was absorbed into the Grand Junction Railway, and then in 1848 the Great Amalgamation took place. Several companies, including the Grand Junction, joined together to form a much larger company called the London and North Western Railway, until the 'grouping' in 1923.

There were in 1922 about a hundred and fifty individual railway companies which, from the beginning of 1923, were grouped into four major companies. The L.N.W.R., the Lancashire and Yorkshire and the Midland Railway now formed the London Midland and Scottish Railway (L.M.S.). Another large group was the London and North Eastern Railway (L.N.E.R.), which included what had formerly been the Great Central Railway in the Manchester area. The other two companies which emerged from the grouping were the Southern Railway (S.R.) and the Great Western Railway (G.W.R.). For more than twenty years the original Liverpool and Manchester Railway continued as part of the L.M.S. system until, on 1 January 1948, the Transport Act put the railways, as well as some other forms of transport, under public ownership. The railways have been nationalised since that date, first as British Railways, and later, after a change of title in 1965, as British Rail. In this way one of the many individual companies found its place in the unified system we have today.

While the Liverpool and Manchester Railway was attracting its own group of smaller connecting lines and gaining access to London via the Grand Junction Railway, in other parts of the country many other lines were being built which linked up with Manchester. As a result of the Industrial Revolution Manchester had grown in importance as the distributing centre for the whole cotton industry of the area. Between 1760 and 1830 the combined population of Manchester and Salford had increased eightfold and in the surrounding area what had once been villages had grown into sizable towns. Also, as the Liverpool and Manchester Railway had its terminus there, Manchester was an even better proposition as the starting point for further lines.

One of these, connecting Lancashire with the great woollen towns east of the Pennines, was the Manchester and Leeds Railway. Once again George Stephenson was the engineer responsible for this formidable undertaking, the first rail crossing of the Pennines. The route he chose took advantage of a natural pass between Littleborough, near Rochdale, and Todmorden at a place called Summit (see Ordnance Survey map 101, grid reference 946182). This pass between the high moors had attracted several forms of transport over the years. The Reddyshore Scout Gate, an old pack-horse route, used the pass and like many old roads it kept to the higher ground. The Rochdale Canal was completed along the lower ground in 1804. In 1824 the turnpike road was constructed near the canal and the last-comer, in 1840, was the railway.

c

The crossing of the Summit Pass proved to be the most difficult part of the line. Stephenson decided to tunnel beneath the pass so that the gradients would not be too great for the none-too-powerful locomotives of the time. The tunnel is 1 mile 1,125 yards long and when completed it was the longest on a railway in the country. Excavation proceeded from fourteen shafts; work went on at thirty separate faces with a labour force of 1,000 men. The cost of the tunnel was £300,000 and twenty-three million bricks were used in its building. The shafts can still be seen today, and if you visit the area from the nearby station at Littleborough, you will see the commemorative stone set in the station wall. The original Manchester terminus of this railway was at what is now the Oldham Road goods depot.

A connection with the Liverpool and Manchester Railway would obviously have been an advantage from the very first but it was only after some reluctance on the part of the Liverpool and Manchester Railway that a connection was eventually made. The Manchester and Leeds line was extended to a new station at Hunt's Bank, called Victoria after the Queen. In 1844 the Liverpool and Manchester Railway was extended to Victoria Station and all the passenger traffic was transferred there, the Liverpool Road Station being made into a goods depot. The Manchester and Leeds Railway became an important part of the Lancashire and Yorkshire Railway and the Liverpool and Manchester, as we have seen, joined the London and North Western Railway.

The L.N.W.R. acquired its own route between Manchester and Leeds in 1849 when a more direct line via Stalybridge and Huddersfield was completed. This line included the notable Standedge Tunnel between Marsden and Diggle. With a length of 3 miles 62 yards it is longer than the old Woodhead Tunnel, opened in 1845 on the Manchester to Sheffield line, by forty yards. The original Standedge tunnel ran parallel to an earlier tunnel of the Huddersfield (narrow)

An express on the Hull, Leeds, Manchester and Liverpool inter-city service emerging from the Diggle end of the Standedge North Tunnel, 1966

Canal, built between 1794 and 1811. The first railway tunnel was single track and in 1870 a second single-track tunnel was opened alongside, and yet another in 1894, a double-track one which indicated the increase of traffic over this route. The tunnels all have water pick-up troughs inside them, an economical scheme for locomotives to collect water at high speed. The troughs are filled with ground-water which has drained into the tunnel. This route is used today by the Liverpool to Newcastle expresses and the Liverpool to Hull Trans-Pennine trains.

In 1880 because the shared station at Victoria had become over-crowded the L.N.W.R. decided to move into its own station adjacent to Victoria. This was called Exchange Station and, at the same time, the Lancashire and Yorkshire undertook the extension of Victoria, which was extended even further in 1904. Victoria Station today has many reminders of its earlier ownership, with its proud frontage and glass panels proclaiming the names of towns to which the railway gave access. Inside is a large wall map showing the extent of the Lancashire

*An English Electric Type 4 diesel locomotive leaves the sunlight
for the gloom of Platform Four at Exchange Station, 1966*

and Yorkshire system before the grouping, characteristically leaving
out the lines of certain rival companies. How many passengers must
have been deceived into taking lengthy and devious journeys as a
result of inter-company rivalry?

The refreshment room at Victoria is well worth a visit as a reminder
of some of the best railway architecture; the ceiling is particularly
interesting. On the station itself the aspect of platforms 12 to 17 is
somewhat bleak, partly due to extensive bomb damage on 23 December
1940. On the previous night Exchange Station lost its adminis-
trative buildings in an air raid and this accounts for its patched-up
appearance today. One feature of the combined stations is what is
claimed as the longest platform in Britain. This begins as platform 3
in Exchange and continues as platform 11 in Victoria, the combined
length being 2,194 feet.

The Manchester and Birmingham Railway, opened in 1842 did not,

Tile mural in the entrance to Victoria Station

in fact, run direct to Birmingham but joined the Grand Junction Railway at Crewe. It became part of the L.N.W.R. at the Great Amalgamation (1848). The original station in Manchester, called London Road after the street where it was built, was renamed Piccadilly in 1960. The station was shared with the Sheffield, Ashton under Lyne and Manchester Railway which started in 1845 as a route to Sheffield via the Woodhead Tunnel. Over the years this railway extended further afield and became known as the Manchester, Sheffield and Lincolnshire Railway. In 1899 it reached London and again changed its title, to the Great Central Railway. By means of the extension it competed for the London traffic by running trains along its own main line to its London terminus at Marylebone but this main line was closed under the Beeching Plan.

The station at London Road was rebuilt in 1865 and again in 1958, in connection with the electrification of the Euston-Manchester line.

The Great Northern Railway's goods warehouse, Deansgate,
with cars parking where tracks formerly were

The whole of the front of the Piccadilly building was pulled down and
replaced by a modern ten-storey office block and two-storey building
housing passenger facilities. The original steelwork of the station roof
has been retained, and the ornamentation and style of this older part
of the station is in sharp contrast with the modern functional part.
Other reminders of the past are a stone water bowl on platform 1
dating back to the earlier rebuilding and a very fine crest of the
Manchester-Birmingham Railway, dated 1839, in the entrance to the
booking offices. The observant passer-by may have noticed the stone
heads of sheep in the gloomy cavern of the Victorian London Road
goods depot.

Nearby is Mayfield Station, opened in 1910 by the L.N.W.R. to
accommodate the overflow traffic from London Road Station but
now only used for freight. The Manchester South Junction and Altrincham Railway also had platforms at London Road. This was a joint
line, shared by the Great Central and L.N.W.R., but the terminus
was moved in 1960 from London Road to Oxford Road as part of

Manchester Central Station

the recent modernisation. Oxford Road is now the terminus of the 25,000-volt Crewe to Manchester service as well as the 1,500-volt Altrincham service in the opposite direction.

Manchester Central is the last of the large stations in Manchester, built in 1880 as the terminal of the Cheshire Lines Committee. In spite of its ambiguous title, this railway was a joint enterprise owned by the Great Central, the Great Northern and the Midland. (The huge warehouse of the Great Northern in Deansgate proudly spells out its origin.) The Cheshire Lines Committee was famous for its fast and punctual trains between Manchester and Liverpool via Warrington and it competed with the L.N.W.R. trains from Exchange and the Lancashire and Yorkshire ones from Victoria. In 1877 the trains from Central Station did the journey to Liverpool in forty-five minutes, the same time as in 1967, and certain trains reduced the time to forty minutes by cutting out the stop at Warrington.

An interesting point about the Cheshire Lines Committee is that it owned no locomotives of its own, although it had its own coaches and rolling stock. The motive power was provided first by the Manchester, Sheffield and Lincolnshire Railway and after the grouping by the L.N.E.R. Manchester Central Station is noted for its fine arch with a span of 210 feet and for the 'temporary' wooden booking offices built when the line was first opened and still in use today. When the grouping took place in 1923 the financial consequences of putting the Cheshire Lines Committee in one of the large companies were so complicated that it was left as an independent concern. Of its joint owners the Midland went into the L.M.S. and the other two companies into the L.N.E.R., but the C.L.C. remained proudly aloof until it was swallowed up with its bigger brethren in the nationalisation of 1948.

A constant reminder of the age of competing companies in Manchester is the inconvenience of having several main-line termini considerable distances apart from each other. Over the years various suggestions have been made to overcome this; in 1912, for example, a tube railway was proposed to circle the central Manchester area, but the plan came to nothing. Another interesting scheme which never materialised was in the 1945 post-war plan for the city and proposed a new station, to be called Trinity, built between the present Salford and Exchange Stations. This would have combined the functions of Central, Victoria and Exchange Stations with connections to London Road and Oxford Road Stations. The Manchester Plan for 1945 prepared for the City Council gives more details of this interesting suggestion.

It is clear from the modernisation and reorganisation now in progress on British Rail that two at least of the present terminals are likely to become redundant. With the pruning away of unprofitable and duplicated services it is probable that the remaining services will be concentrated into fewer termini. It would be interesting to collect press cuttings concerning the many future changes in our local railways.

A public Notice of Closure. This station on the main line from Manchester to Sheffield opened in August 1844 and was closed in March 1964

5 The changing scene

History is a continuous process and is taking place now. In no field is this more evident than in transport. Many people alive now grew up in an age when the express train represented the ultimate in man's quest for speed. Today, when rockets and orbital spacecraft are becoming common, the railways themselves are undergoing vast changes. If we remember that in the early years of the railways the rival forms of transport were the horse and cart and the canal barge, we can understand why today the railways have so much to do in adapting themselves to modern conditions.

The main theme of these changes was outlined in the Beeching Report (called after its author Dr Richard Beeching), *The Reshaping of British Railways*, published in 1963. This report analyses the future role of the railways and makes plans to run them on a more economic footing; briefly, the plan is to reduce those operations for which the railways are not suited and to develop those for which they are. In this way it is hoped to cut down the increasing losses made by the nationalised railways, which weigh more and more heavily on the British tax-payer.

One aspect of the plan is the withdrawal of many passenger services which are little used or which run at a heavy loss. These services originated in the days when there were no other convenient forms of transport and people were dependent on the railways for going to work or to market each day. With the coming of the electric tram at the end of the nineteenth century and then the motor bus, the use of railways for local travelling rapidly declined. It is much easier to board a bus passing through the centre of a town or village than to walk, often a considerable distance, to the nearest railway station, which, for geographical reasons, might be built away from the centre of population. Buses are also more suitable for carrying smaller numbers of passengers at more frequent intervals and since people have a shorter time to wait between buses, this again gives the advantage to buses over trains. As fewer people use the trains, the trains become less frequent and this in itself makes the residual service less popular. Again, the railway is less flexible than road transport. Very often a slow stopping train cannot be run at what would be the best time from the passengers' point of view because at this time it would block the line and obstruct the running of other more important long-distance trains.

The Beeching Report, therefore, proposes to withdraw passenger services from 605 miles of railway in the north-western lines area. This is about one-third of the total of the area and involves the closure of about three hundred stations, about half the total. For the remaining services the Report recommends the substitution of diesel or electric traction for steam to provide faster and more reliable services. According to the Report the cost per train mile for steam locomotive-hauled trains is about fifteen shillings whereas the cost of diesel multiple units is only 4s. 6d. according to the density of the traffic.

A train on the reprieved Manchester to Buxton line,
alongside the abandoned Peak Forest Tramway, 1963

Understandably the proposals to withdraw services and close local stations have aroused some opposition, particularly from those who, without trains, would have to travel by the slower bus or private car. This is a very real problem in the Manchester area, aggravated by the congested road conditions in and around the city, particularly in the morning and evening peak hours. Before any railway passenger service can be withdrawn, however, details must be published in advance. Then, if any objections are made by the users of the service within a certain period of time, an inquiry is held by a body called the Transport Users Consultative Committee who look into any possible hardship which would be caused if the service were withdrawn and report their findings to the Minister of Transport who makes the final decision. Sometimes it is decided to retain a service, as with the Buxton to Manchester Piccadilly line. This line, opened in 1863, climbs up to Buxton via Stockport and Whaley Bridge through hilly country where road conditions are often very bad in winter snow and where the journey by rail is much quicker than by road. In other cases the Minister, believing that the economies resulting outweigh any possible hardship, has ordered the closure to take place. The Glaze-brook-Wigan Central branch is an example, although the withdrawal was made subject to the provision of additional bus services and that the track between Glazebrook and Lowton St Mary's should not be lifted without the Minister's consent. The Wigan branch was formerly owned by the Great Central Railway and was opened in 1879, originally built to carry coal from the mines at Bickershaw and West Leigh.

These local closures are not a new departure; they have, in fact, been going on for some time. Many stations in this area were closed before the Beeching Report, some because of changing local conditions like that at Crowden in the Longdendale Valley on the Manchester-Sheffield electrified line, closed in 1957. This derelict station can be seen by Youth Hostellers who visit the new hostel nearby, opened in 1965. A much larger station closed in 1954 was the one at Bolton in Great Moor Street, because trains on the former L.N.W.R. route were duplicated by the more frequent service on the Lancashire and Yorkshire line from Trinity Street Station close by. This station at Great Moor Street is famous because in 1858 the original stone station was completely destroyed by a runaway train of thirty-two loaded wagons hauled by an engine named *Redstart* which got out of control down the 1:48 gradient approach. The train ended up beyond the station in the middle of Great Moor Street.

With the fast and semi-fast inter-city train services the picture is quite different as many of these make a substantial contribution to the railway finances and it is intended to increase this by providing faster and more comfortable services and so attract more passengers. Selected stations are being modernised; for example, Stalybridge has recently had a facelift which improves its appearance considerably from the

The first Manchester Pullman on arrival at Manchester Piccadilly, 18 April 1966

street. Modern methods of issuing tickets can be seen at Piccadilly. An example of the enterprising way in which the railways can come to terms with the competition from the private car is the high-speed car-carrier service introduced in 1965 between Newton le Willows and Stirling. A daily train leaves Newton, equidistant from both Manchester and Liverpool, carrying the motor-cars on special carflats, while the motorists travel in de luxe passenger accommodation in the same train, avoiding the long tedious drive to northern Scotland.

An example of British Rail being at the forefront of modern techno-logical development is the Manchester-Euston electrification scheme. This is virtually a completely new railway designed for trains speeding at 100 miles per hour. Power is provided from overhead wires at 25,000 volts A.C. collected from a pantograph on the roof of the locomotive. An electricity supply at this voltage, over a hundred times that of an ordinary mains supply, has to be adequately insulated. Actual contact with the wire is not necessary for a short circuit to take place as the current can jump several inches. Between Manchester and Crewe eighty-two of the ninety-two bridges over the track had to be rebuilt or radically altered. In addition, to safeguard trains travelling at 100 miles per hour, modern multiple-aspect colour signalling had to be provided. At Piccadilly one can see from the platforms the new power-operated signal box controlling the sections from Levenshulme and Gatley to Piccadilly. This box now does the work formerly done by twelve of the old-type signal boxes.

Freight traffic is important to the economics of the railway and the Beeching Report plans changes here as well. Instead of about five thousand freight depots up and down the country the Report suggests only a few hundred. Formerly each depot had to be within horse and cart distance of the customer, but now, with efficient road transport, traders can afford rather longer distances for collection and delivery. In the north-western lines area, 391 out of a total of 561 goods depots are due for closure, many of these being wayside depots serving village communities. Another economy is the aim of the railways to deal as far as possible with complete trainloads which do not require shunting en route but run as a complete, or block, train. It is proposed to close many of the small coal depots and replace them with fewer concentration coal depots. These could be served by complete trainloads of coal at a time from a single colliery. One very successful block train already running carries limestone from the quarries at Tunstead in the Peak District to the I.C.I. Alkaline Division at Northwich. Each of these trains consists of sixteen or seventeen fully fitted 46-ton steel bogie wagons and they run continually between the two places carrying one and a half million tons annually.

Block train of I.C.I. hopper wagons coming out of
Dove Holes Tunnel towards Tunstead, 1964

Another scheme, intended to make the most of the joint use of road and rail transport is the plan for liner trains. These carry merchandise from door to door in standard containers using road transport to railheads at selected centres. At one of these, in Manchester, containers are loaded by special equipment on to fast liner trains of low flat wagons. These travel at high speeds along trunk routes to another centre where they are rapidly unloaded and taken by road to their destination. For distances over a hundred miles the costs of this service are calculated to be less than that for overall road transport. The liner trains are never shunted, but run as continuous trains between the different centres. The Speedfreight service is a forerunner of the liner trains. This train runs at high speed overnight, both ways between Manchester and London, and gives next-day delivery from the modernised Ardwick South goods station, using large aluminium containers which are transferred to road vehicles for the last part of the journey. An extension of this kind of freight service will eliminate the need for so many marshalling yards; at present there are still seventeen round Manchester. It is claimed that with modernised working all but two could be dispensed with.

Modernisation has also affected the railway workshops. Previously each of the major companies had its own workshops where they built their own locomotives and rolling stock, etc. This was uneconomic when the railways were organised as one concern, so some of the large workshops have been run down or closed completely. One of these, closed in 1963, was at Gorton where the works of the former Great Central Railway employed 1,400 men. The powerful EM2 electric locomotives which run between Manchester and Sheffield were built here. The Lancashire and Yorkshire works were at Horwich, but the construction and repair of locomotives ceased in 1964; this works is used for repairing electric multiple units and wagons (once repaired at the Earlestown works of the former L.N.W.R., now closed).

Part of the Gorton locomotive works just before closure in 1963

From
The Guardian,
May 1963

At present great changes are taking place on the railways and it is quite certain that many more will come in the future. Some people regret the passing of the old order, and look back with nostalgia to the era when the steam engine reigned supreme. This emotion is probably felt in any period of change. When the railways came, there were those who mourned the passing of the stage-coach. Possibly, if electrification proves to be superior, there will be people in a few decades' time mourning the passing of the diesel. The value of a local history study is that one can interest oneself in the present and have the knowledge to view it in the perspective of the past, so that one is able to see the relationship between the past and the present. In this way we can realise that much of what exists today is inherited from past generations and that the progress of today is founded on the past.

Electric train entering the new Woodhead Tunnel, opened in 1954

Anyone interested in the history of railways will never be at a loss for something to do. A few suggestions are made in this chapter to give some idea of the variety of interests available. It is not the point at which you start which is important. The depth of interest arises not in answer to the first question, but in where you are led as you discover more. An alert person will notice many curiosities which invite questions. This is particularly so now that one can see the journey through the front window of a diesel unit with a view along the track that one never had a few years ago. How many people, on a journey between Manchester and Bolton, notice that each of the two lines has a separate tunnel at Farnworth and wonder why the two tunnels are of different sizes? There are many interesting things to be discovered about the history of particular places. How many people, as they pass through the prosaic station at Clifton today, know the fascinating story of the Battle of Clifton Junction?

The battle arose as a result of the rivalry between the East Lancashire and the Lancashire and Yorkshire railways. In 1849 the main line between Manchester and Bolton was owned by the L. & Y. and the branch which turns off northwards at Clifton was owned by the E.L. railway. The E.L. trains used the L. & Y. line from Clifton into Manchester for its Bury to Manchester trains, but had to pay a toll to the L. & Y. based on the number of passengers on these trains. The L. & Y. checked this by making the trains stop at Clifton Junction where they collected the tickets and counted the passengers. It occurred to the E.L. company that their service would be improved if they ran straight through Clifton without stopping and just informed

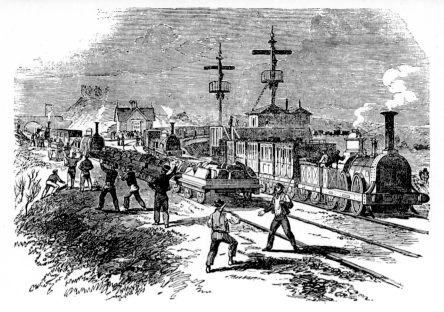

The scene at Clifton in 1849

the L. & Y. company how many people there were on their trains. They even offered to allow the L. & Y. company to see their books if they wished. The L. & Y. were having nothing to do with this and when the E.L. railway insisted on running their trains through Clifton Junction without stopping the L. & Y. took action. When the first E.L. train was due on Monday, 12 March, the L. & Y. blocked the track with a huge baulk of timber and to make doubly sure brought up a train of their own to block the track to Manchester. The E.L. train was forced to stop and a gang of E.L. men came along to remove the obstacle. Then, with a strong force of county police standing by in case of violence, the E.L. train drew forward and attempted to force the L. & Y. train out of the way. This was impossible as by now the L. & Y. had brought up an extra engine to help on their side. The E.L. retaliated by running a stone ballast train on to the junction to block the line in the other direction so that L. & Y. trains could not travel the down line from Manchester to Bolton. More and more trains kept arriving during the morning until eight different trains were jammed around the junction. By now it was dinner time and the L. & Y. officials went off for a meal leaving a certain Mr Blackhouse in charge of the battle. Mr Blackhouse decided that the time had come to use a little common sense. His first action was to order his forces to retreat and soon the lines were cleared. Later the Treaty of Manchester was negotiated by which East Lancashire's trains were allowed to pass through Clifton Junction without stopping.

One problem is how to get the information for a local study, or to answer a particular question. A list of some of the books useful for our area is given on pages 62-3. If a particular book is not in your library, the librarian will be pleased to obtain it for you. For more detailed information there are files on various aspects of the railways in the Local History Section of the Manchester Central Library. These include newspaper cuttings going back many years. In the Central Library one can consult bound volumes of the *Railway Magazine* and other periodicals in some cases dating back to the construction of the railways. Files or microfilms of newspapers and periodicals are also available in many local libraries. Your local library should have copies of local papers, useful for the study of a particular area. Some local museums have material and information valuable to the railway historian. How complex the pre-grouping system of the railways was can be seen from the one-inch O.S. map, sheet 101, of Manchester, especially if the lines of each company are traced in a different colour on to a large sheet of paper. Notice the radial nature of the lines, being attracted towards Manchester as if drawn by a giant magnet. See the way that certain companies dominated particular areas, the Lancashire and Yorkshire in the North, and the London and North Western in two distinct areas; you will remember that this company also had two main-line termini in Manchester. Notice how the Great Central coming in over the Pennines from

Sheffield was able to penetrate with the help of joint lines to Wigan, Liverpool, Southport and other towns. Observe also the Midland sneaking into Manchester via Chinley from the centre of its web at Derby. The *British Railways Pre-grouping Atlas and Gazetteer* will be found a great help.

In drawing maps or studying the history of railways one soon comes across the many cryptic initials of the early companies. The earlier one goes the more prolific these become. By reference to various histories a list can be compiled of the names and initials of the companies in this area. You will find that some of the titles were rather misleading. The Cheshire Lines Committee, for example, had most of its lines, including the main Manchester to Liverpool line, in Lancashire rather than Cheshire. But the name is sometimes a clue to the early origin of the railway, as with the Manchester Bolton and Bury Canal Navigation and Railway. On a journey from Manchester to Bolton today one can see, at least as far as Clifton Junction, the close relationship between the two forms of transport at one time under the same management.

This relationship between the railway and other forms of transport is an interesting study in itself. At the Bury Canal Quay, for example, well away from the railway, is a stone in the wall on the main road a few yards from the entrance with the initials of the Manchester, Bolton and Bury Canal Navigation and Railway. The stone is set into the wall at foot level and it is likely that many people have walked within inches of it over the years and never noticed it, and at the rate at which it is being eroded, those who fail to see it soon are never likely to. A little nearer to the entrance is a more recent Lancashire and Yorkshire notice, and on a building just inside, a cast-iron plate shows that the London Midland and Scottish Railway finally inherited the quay.

Railway notices themselves may be well worth a study. There are many to be seen, particularly around some of the older stations and by the lineside at level crossings and where footpaths cross the track. Usually they are made of cast iron with raised letters and they were obviously intended to last a long time. They are often headed with the name or initials of the railway company. Where they are accessible they form interesting subjects for brass rubbing techniques using heel ball and white paper, though in all cases you should obtain the permission of the station master unless the notice is on public land.

Look out for old postcards depicting railway scenes. Many of the early companies published cards showing views on the railways which are of interest to the local historian; for example, the London and North Western Railway had published over five million by 1906. Some were used for official business mail, and some were even given away for publicity purposes, as for example on the Great Central dining cars. Many were produced then, as now, by commercial firms. These cards occasionally turn up in jumble sales and if so they should be carefully preserved. Sometimes one comes across them in old bookshops, for example on the bookstalls at Shudehill.

Old railway timetables form a fascinating study for the historian. Timetables are usually thrown away when they are out of date and for that reason the older ones particularly are very scarce. If you come across an old timetable it should be looked after very carefully, not only for its historical interest, but because it might also have considerable monetary value. Timetables were not only produced by the individual companies; they were also published by other authorities, sometimes to cover the whole country. The most celebrated became known as a Bradshaw after its originator. George Bradshaw was born at Pendleton in 1801 and in 1821 he established a printing business in Manchester which is still operating under the name of Henry Blacklock & Co., Ltd. He specialised in the printing of maps, showing roads and canals, and then later railways. He produced the earliest known railway timetables in 1839, though he may have printed some in 1838 which have never been discovered. The great advantage of Bradshaw's timetables was that they covered the whole country, showing the times of all the different companies. They were published at intervals until the final issue of May, 1961. Publication ceased through the competition of the cheaper regional timetables of British Railways, though if you look on the back page of the London Midland Region timetable of British Rail (1968) you will find that it has been printed by Henry Blacklock & Co. of Bradshaw House, Manchester. A copy of the first Bradshaw is in the Rylands Library in Manchester. The early timetables not only give details of the train services but often insights into the social and economic conditions of the time. In a timetable for 1837, *Cornish's Grand Junction and Liverpool and Manchester Railway Companion*, price 1s. od., we find among the regulations – 'Passengers intending to join the trains at any of the stopping places are desired to be in good time, as the train will leave each station as soon as ready without reference to the time mentioned in the tables, the main object being to perform the whole journey as expeditiously as possible.'

Railway buildings form another possible topic for study. Some date from the earliest period, such as Earlestown and Rainhill on the Liverpool and Manchester line. Others, even though they might appear to be of great antiquity to the modern traveller, were rebuilt at a comparatively recent date. For example, the original station at Bolton was built in 1848, but it was rebuilt in 1904. It will be observed that certain features tend to be repeated along the stations of a particular company. This applies not only to the major construction of buildings and station awnings but also to smaller things like lamps, seats and footbridges. The same applies to many lineside features associated with the railway, such as mile-posts, signals and signal boxes. There are many signal boxes around Manchester dating back well into the

Sheffield, Ashton-under-Lyne & Manchester.

GODLEY TO MANCHESTER	a.m	a.m	a.m	a.m	p.m	p.m	p.m	p.m	p.m	p.m	Fares.		
											1 Clss.	2 Clss.	3 Clss.
Godley	8 0	9 0	10 0	11 0	1 0	3 0	4 0	5 0	7 0	7 45	s. d.	s. d.	s. d.
Newton	9 5	9 5	10 5	11 5	1 5	3 5	4 5	5 5	7 5	7 50	0 3	0 2	0 2
Dukinfield	8 12	9 12	10 12	11 12	1 12	3 12	4 12	5 12	7 12	7 57	0 6	0 4	0 3
Ashton	8 17	9 17	10 17	11 17	1 17	3 17	4 17	5 17	7 17	8 2	0 8	0 5	0 4
Fairfield........	8 24	9 24	10 24	11 24	1 24	3 24	4 24	5 24	7 24	8 9	1 0	0 8	0 6
Manchester	8 32	9 32	10 32	11 32	1 32	3 32	4 32	5 32	7 32	8 17	1 6	1 2	0 10

MANCHESTER TO GODLEY	a.m	a.m	a.m.	noon	p.m	p.m	p.m	p.m	p.m	p.m.	1 Clss.	2 Clss.	3 Clss.
Manchester	9 0	10 0	11 0	12 0	2 0	4 0	5 0	6 0	7 45	8 45	s. d.	s. d.	s. d.
Fairfield........	9 11	10 11	11 11	12 11	2 11	4 11	5 11	6 11	7 56	8 56	0 8	0 6	0 4
Ashton	9 18	10 18	11 18	12 18	2 18	4 18	5 18	6 18	8 3	9 3	1 0	0 9	0 6
Dukinfield	9 22	10 22	11 22	12 22	2 22	4 22	5 22	6 22	8 7	9 7	1 0	0 9	0 6
Newton	9 30	10 30	11 30	12 30	2 30	4 30	5 30	6 30	8 15	9 15	1 3	1 0	0 8
Godley	9 32	10 32	11 32	12 32	2 32	4 32	5 32	6 32	8 17	9 17	1 6	1 2	0 0

Sunday Trains.—From Manchester to Godley, at 9 & 10 a.m., and 7, 8, & 8 40 p.m. From Godley to Manchester, at 8 & 9 a.m., and 5 45, 7, & 8 p.m. All mixed, and stopping at all the stations.

N.B.—Each passenger allowed 60lbs. of Luggage, free of charge. The fares to the intermediate stations are charged in proportion to the distances from the starting points. Parcels may be booked at the above named stations at the following rates :—For parcels under 14lbs. 6d.; from 14lbs. to 28lbs. 9d. 28lbs. to 56lbs.; 1s.; 56lbs. to 112lbs. 1s. 6d. An additional penny on every 8lbs. Dogs with passengers, 3d.—The Booking Office is for the present at the temporary station of the Manchester and Birmingham Railway Company, in Travis-street.

Extract from a Bradshaw of 1842 when construction had only reached Godley

pre-grouping days, and each one characteristic of the company that built it. As one travels the route of the old Great Central Railway from the Woodhead Tunnel towards Manchester past characteristic G.C. signal boxes (apart from one or two more recent modern types, – Hadfield, Woodhead, for example), the sight of a typical Midland Railway box beyond Ashburys indicates that at one time there was Midland Railway influence there. In fact at one time the line branching to the right was used by the Midland Railway to obtain access to Manchester Victoria Station. This is part of the intriguing story of how the Midland Railway penetrated into Manchester. Many bridges have plates on them giving the date of their construction and the name of the builder. The highly ornamental nature of some of the bridges is well worth a study. On the lines out of Manchester Central the railway arches with their ornamental turrets are a good example.

Stations and lineside features are also of considerable interest to the many people who model railways in a historical setting. These enthusiasts need not buy all their material ready made, but derive

Royal Scot Commemorative tour organised by the Railway
Correspondence and Travel Society, stopped at Wigan, February 1965

pleasure from creating a model which represents accurately the railway at a given period. Several magazines catering for this interest are listed in the appendix. Some of the models now in existence have great historical value as they will survive long after the original has been scrapped.

In many places the railway has already outlived its usefulness, and in others where it has disappeared little remains to indicate its former glory. Stations are gone, the track lifted and the land reintegrated into the life of the area, and yet their influence remains with us. Many towns and villages owe their present life and prosperity to the trade brought by the railway. Yet in some places the only link remaining might, in the future, be the oddly placed inn with a name like The Railway Hotel, The Station Arms, or The Midland. These, in future years, will no doubt join The Wagon and Horses and The Coachman's Arms as places with a hint of the old-fashioned and quaint. In fact here is yet another subject waiting to be studied, either from the outside or from the inside, according to the age of the student.

Appendix A Facilities offered by British Rail

British Rail maintain three major collections of historic interest.

1) *The Railway Museum at York*
This is the most accessible for this area and is situated near York station. It is in two sections. The Large Exhibits Section houses locomotives, ranging from one built by George Stephenson as early as 1822 to steam giants that were still in use on express trains well into this century. Also included are wagons, signals, parts of bridges and other large objects. In the Small Exhibits Section is a fine collection of early pictures and prints as well as all manner of other relics such as clocks, batons, buttons, bells and curiosities along with many beautifully constructed models. The Museum is open on weekdays between 10 a.m. and 5 p.m. Admission to the Small Exhibits is free, the charge to the Large Exhibits is 1s. for adults and 6d. for children. It is worth while for the leader of a party to write beforehand to The Curator, Railway Museum, York, as material is available for the preparation of topic books.

2) *The Great Western Museum at Swindon*
Further particulars are available from The Curator, G.W.R. Museum, Swindon, Wiltshire.

3) *The Museum of British Transport at Clapham*
This museum includes other forms of transport and particulars may be obtained from The Curator, Museum of British Transport, Clapham High Street, London SW4.

Films and filmstrips

British Rail have an extensive library of films and filmstrips available free on loan, some of interest from a historical viewpoint. The film catalogue is priced 5s. 0d. and the filmstrip catalogue 2s. 6d. They can both be obtained from The Chief Officer, Films, British Railways Board, 25 Savile Row, London W1.

Projection equipment and projectionists can sometimes be made available to present a complete programme to suitable audiences.

Visits to railway installations

Subject to certain conditions British Rail allow visits to motive power depots and works, and by prior arrangement parties are occasionally taken round special locations such as the original station in Liverpool Road. For information concerning visits in this area application should be made to The Divisional Public Relations Officer, Hunt's Bank, Manchester 3.

Publications

The British Railways Board has produced a 'Rail Facts for Teachers' pack, containing a book, leaflets, maps, photographs, and charts. This has been distributed free to secondary schools. For details of this and other publications the address is British Railways Board, Public Relations Division, 222 Marylebone Road, London NW1.

Appendix B Societies

Societies

There are many societies catering for the railway enthusiast, some having branches active in the North-west. These range from clubs

60

which organise motor-coach tours to motive power depots to satisfy the needs of the number-takers, to those like the Railway and Canal Historical Society where papers of very high scholarship are read.

The names and addresses of the secretaries of the various clubs and societies can be found in the periodicals given in Appendix C, though most of the larger societies have an adult membership. One society however with a nominal age limit of 16 does make special provision for 14–15 year olds. This is the Railway Correspondence and Travel Society which caters for the average enthusiast. The society publishes a monthly magazine and details of membership along with a specimen copy of the magazine can be obtained by sending 6d. in stamps to The Hon. Secretary, 82 Natal Road, New Southgate, London N11.

Like several other societies the R.C.T.S. organises frequent rail tours over lines of historic interest. These are usually open to non-members and advertised in the railway magazines. Valuable features of many of these in the past have been the well produced itineraries and maps giving details of the histories of the lines travelled.

Youth Hostels Association
The Youth Hostels Association have for some time organised Eagle adventure holidays especially designed for the age group 11–15. Those for railway enthusiasts are run in conjunction with British Rail and an expert guide is present to show the many aspects of railway life. During 1966 two such courses were held, in Yorkshire and Devon. The inclusive cost for the week was £9 15s. od. Details of future courses may be obtained from The Youth Hostels Association, Home Tours Department, Trevelyan House, St Albans, Herts.

Appendix C Some books for further reference

Biography
ROLT, L. T. C. *George and Robert Stephenson* Longmans, 1960.
SMILES, SAMUEL *Life of George Stephenson* John Murray, 1864.

Individual Railway Companies
BASNET, LOIS *The First Public Railway in Lancashire* Lancashire and
  Cheshire Antiquarian Society, 1963 (The Bolton and Leigh Railway).
CHADWICK, STANLEY *'All stations to Manchester': the Centenary of the
  Huddersfield and Manchester Railway and Standedge Tunnel* Venturers
  Press, 1949.
DENDY MARSHALL, C. E. *The Centenary History of the Liverpool and Man-
  chester Railway* Locomotive Publishing Company, 1930.
DOW, GEORGE *Great Central* (3 vols.) Locomotive Publishing Company,
  1959–65.
ELLIS, HAMILTON *The Midland Railway* Ian Allan, 1953.
GRIFFITHS, R. P. *The Cheshire Lines Railway* Oakwood Press, 1958.
HOLT, GEOFFREY OGDEN *A Short History of the Liverpool and Manchester
  Railway* Railway and Canal Historical Society, 1965 (2nd edn).
MASON, E. *The Lancashire and Yorkshire Railway in the Twentieth Century*
  Ian Allan, 1954.
NOCK, O. S. *The London and North Western Railway* Ian Allan, 1960.
RIMMER, A. *The Cromford and High Peak Railway* Oakwood Press, 1956.

General
BLOWER, ALAN *British Railway Tunnels* Ian Allan, 1964.
BRITISH RAILWAYS BOARD *The Reshaping of British Railways* H.M.S.O. 1963.
  The Development of Major Railway Trunk Routes London: H.M.S.O. 1965.
CONOLLY, W. PHILIP *British Railways Pre-grouping Atlas and Gazetteer*
  Railway Publications (no date).

62

COLEMAN, TERRY   *The Railway Navvies*   Hutchinson, 1965. (Contains a first rate account of the boring of the Woodhead Tunnels.)

ELLIS, HAMILTON   *British Railway History, 1830–1876*, and *British Railway History, 1877–1947* (2 vols.) George Allen & Unwin, 1954–9.

GREVILLE, M. D.   'Chronological list of the railways of Cheshire 1837–1939' In *Transactions of the Historic Society of Lancashire and Cheshire Vol. 106, 1955.*

GREVILLE, M. D.   'Chronological list of the railways of Lancashire 1828–1939' In *Transactions of the Historic Society of Lancashire and Cheshire Vol. 105, 1953.*

HARRISON, WILLIAM   'History of the Manchester Railways'   Reprinted from *Manchester City News, Notes and Queries*, Vol. IV, 1881–2, by the Lancashire and Cheshire Antiquarian Society, 1967.

HORTON, HARRY   'Some sources of railway history'   In *Manchester Review* Summer 1954 (Manchester Libraries Committee Quarterly Journal).

JACKMAN, W. T.   *The Development of Transportation in Modern England* Frank Cass, 1962 (revised). (This is a weighty volume of profound scholarship; it is interesting to read and gives a balanced comparative account showing the relationship of railways with other forms of transport.)

SIMMONS, JACK   *The Railways of Britain*   Routledge & Kegan Paul, 1961.

Periodicals

The Journal of Transport History is published twice yearly by the University of Leicester.

Modern Railways, published monthly, describes the contemporary scene.

Modern Transport, published monthly, gives information on all forms of transport.

Railway Gazette, published twice monthly, established in 1835, has a world wide coverage.

Railway Magazine, published monthly, describes the contemporary scene and also contains articles of historical interest.

Railway World, published monthly, has a mainly historical bias.

The Model Engineer, Model Railway News and the *Railway Modeller*, all published monthly, are valuable sources of information on railway architecture and equipment.

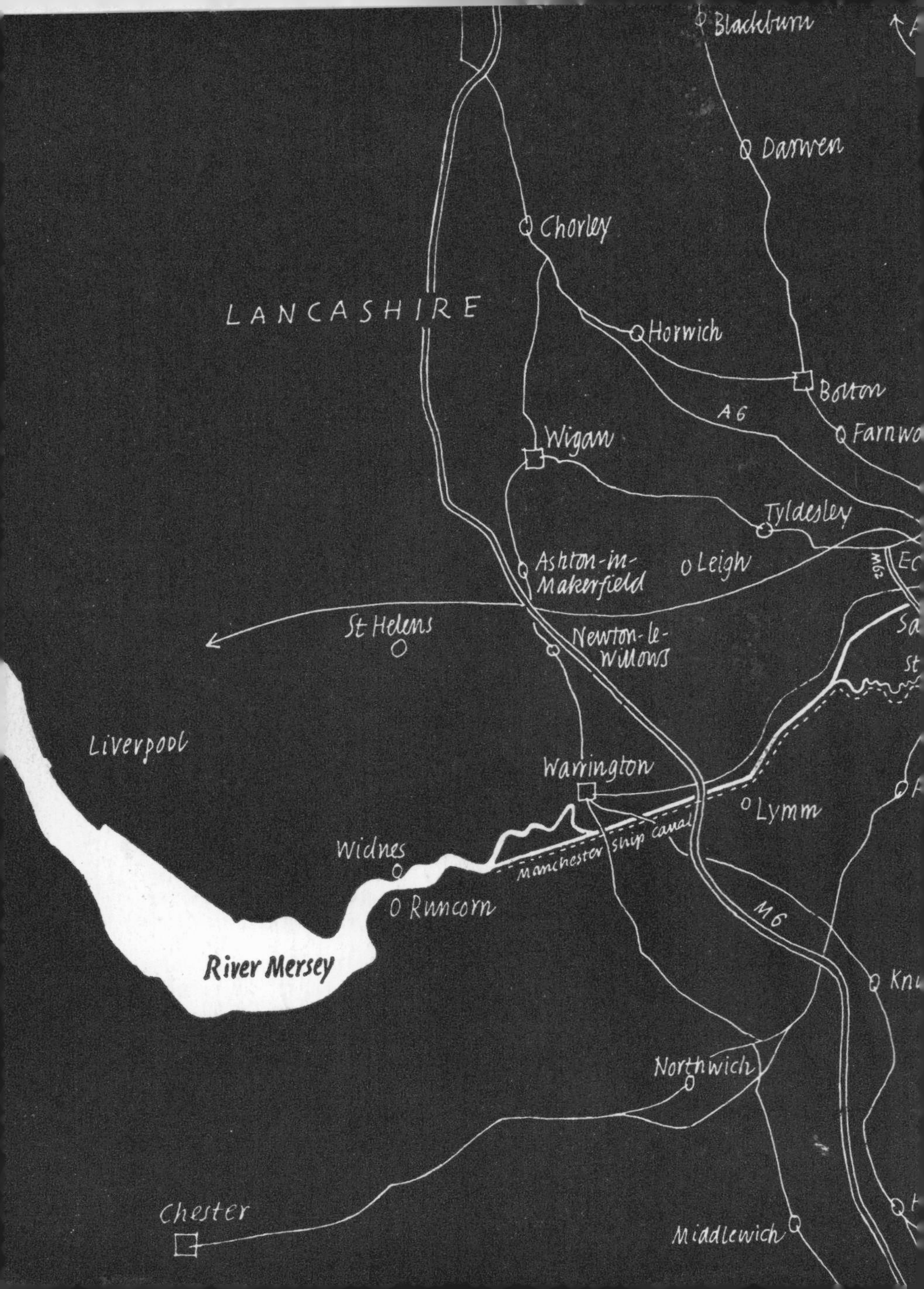

Blackburn

Darwen

Chorley

LANCASHIRE

Horwich

Bolton

A 6

Farnwo

Wigan

Tyldesley

Ashton-in-
Makerfield

o Leigh

EC

M 6 2

St Helens

Newton-le-
Willows

Sa

St

Liverpool

Warrington

Lymm

Widnes

Manchester ship canal

O Runcorn

M 6

River Mersey

Kn

Northwich

Chester

Miadlewich

H